Intaglio Daughters

Intaglio Daughters

Laynie Browne

ORNITHOPTER PRESS   PRINCETON

First Edition

Published by Ornithopter Press
www.ornithopterpress.com

ISBN 978-1-942723-15-8

Library of Congress Control Number: 2023935777

Cover image:
Foxstool, oil on panel, 2022
by Jacob Davidson
courtesy of the artist

Design and composition by Mark Harris

for Lyn Hejinian

Intaglio Daughters

1

The streets are walked by she who fully backwards walks them emptily

Long ago there stood in the midst of a country covered with lakes

a vast stretch of moorland, with worn covers possibly bent

pages stained on edges foxed, yet all text remained visible

Tales with torn ends followed, where falsehoods

became persons. When entirely spent we put our hands

in our sockets and continued following what we imagined

were the steps you might have taken. I had no intention

of continuing to write elegies yet every night I dreamed

of finding you inside a locket circumscribed by this wood

An empty envelope, even when cast in gold is not the threshold

Two drops of water, a cloak and mussel shell are not the sea

or the sack bigger than oneself being dragged into dark

The sheets are stalked by she who fully lacks words, and locks them credibly

2

When love can't be composed any better, then love can't be postponed any longer

Honey lay ankle deep in the valley and knee deep in the hills

In the Fall that never happened mittens fell from trees

We hung our shoes in the eaves, strung spikes from eyes

At the window you thanked me for swallowing pennies

Though I clung to your form by night, by day your voice

thrown sweltering into a pot, afflicted me

Drops of water on my page bled and tore

The sky was flat grey and trees all in flame

During these times we carried our heads about in hat boxes

and put them on only when absolutely necessary

Silence was shackled sleep in the valley and plea swept in chills

We had no need for caps or courtesy, as all thought was kept warmly stowed

When love can't be dethroned any better than love can't be disarmed any longer

3

Time's retraction brings the failure of action

Do you see this girl? I wish to adopt her as my daughter
Make me a copy we can send to her village
Which is worse—to ask for help or to drown?
I signaled to my love through a window locked against fathoms
He saw me but waved me away. With the bone
of a finger I was transcribed into rain, imprecise scribbles
sorrier than verbiage, easier than spent. He was lecturing
to a rabbit: 'Easy to send out a line, impossible to retrieve it'
Do you see this pearl? I wish to drink her like water
I cannot tell you whether the journey is long or short
When asked to alter silence we broke into song
Like the contusion which is violet ushering dusk
Sublime contraction brings derailed subtraction

4

The phrase, this stream, among wolves

The mussel shell and the fish scales were put back in the box

and the girls went in

The lettering was smaller than I thought

I did not rise to meet him, nor did I

greet the red scarf around his neck

He had used himself up

You could tell as the color left his eyes

then hands then mouth

I danced with every version of myself unpardoned

by the satin conversation of your lips

I gave myself to an engraved cover, opening doors

We were a solid wreck darning the word 'darling'

this phase, this seam against resolve

5

The blushing sun has set

He took up a handful of clay and made a doll as large as strife
The book was very tall, taller by one head, with
fingers peeking over the edge and mead streaming out
Like walks, alone, where dreams disturb neighbors
To follow where nothing leads is to emerge from the lake
with no bed, a snapping turtle with leeches on its back
on the way to the opera knowing sound from inside
Earlier was inward and afterward a message
bathed in blue light. A millet seed dropped into the sea
grown before eyes, cut by an invisible hand, made into cake
Lists were erupting from paper, mouths, lasers
Streets disappeared, wombs lurched at a glance
the crushing one has sent

6

Let us go then, you and I, in pajamas through the sky

The conductor's hands waved ice

When the violinist stomped was that scored?

My hair was very long

When I stood it reached the floor

When I sat it reached the eaves

Your tale is as long as your tongue may fly

Wait—let me rearrange your decades

Will you help me to reverse my premises?

And so we undid the clock

and so we unhooked your cloak, and lay it on the ground

amid roving dapples and flecks of velvet light

we may transform ourselves into balls of fire

Let us flow then, you and I, through docudramas in the 'why'

Bird of daughters, bird flying from the forks

The soloist is the main character. She offers
a reprieve from language composed at high elevations
No two shrouds are the same and yet we recognize
clouds as moments without melody, scalloped arks
I press each word to your lip with my own (it's called kissing)
an excursion to the woods after a rain, every leaf reverberant
Not only perplexity traced on paper, but sound
complete and unabridged, including original illustrations
desks scratching and writhing, answers blue and bodily
whip, rod and verbena. *Werb*, turn or bend, branches
of an echo. How to leave marks in a listener's mind
blank words five times fast. How to live in unison; how to coax
unheard of waters, slurred untying of harps

8

Window a red chocolate

What do you know of the bowed voice

of conversing in color, skeins of intuitive neumes?

In your words I dressed and rose

then joined spectral women at a long wooden syntax

though I could not convince myself to be one of them

Snow became silence, your name in more than one language

      pressed into a bed of cotton

Music, that lake which fixes the mind: affix, unfix fixity

Blue violet falls, follows, halos

after the dust of us: after the dusk of loss

unfollows each night—separated as we are from sky

I love you, she said, coming out of the cabinet

where it never rained, but she found no help

nor cinders nor gauntlet

9

Smoke is the noun for the thing over fire

With the eye of a leaf we shall not squander
He bored a hole in the doll's heart, daubed blood inside
I clutched my perfect weakness, black cohosh
in amber glass, gold infusion of sage
Put on my burnished fingers wearing sweaters
gifted from the dead, a drain image, shiny
She began collecting garments stiff enough to stand
on their own without bodies, cells she could not yet know
Enacting a rhyme unaware until several
dream selves in parenthesis followed
I could not retrieve my breath
Weightless to the forest for what I was waiting
Choked or drowned as a wing over mire

10

Night on our faces (for we have many)

Dusk covered leaves, illuminated asides
and every note scrawled. Come closer
into my carriage, my misfortune, my drawstring
hearth. We have entered the opposite
side of each minute. Inside my bag of silence
is time not congealed, nor stroked by light
Where the leaves have only blemished adventures
unspoken ochre or lace, a perfect backdrop
Why must we translate lower and lowered
into the ground. The dead are not voiceless
You were not a stone mother, a scrap landscape
If only I loved anyone as I loved blankness and
the emptiness in my possession, lull and darkness
Flight in our embraces (for we have plenty)

11

Reason what of flurry, what of fishes, of fury

Where no words console, sustenance is the relentless
search for your other—us, us! A heaven of silk fitting
two words together, through pencil lines of
hair, nests, puzzles of hands securing the page
Once arrived at the pond I rejected an entire oeuvre
of migraines, the skin of a frog, its toes brushed my
lip then shoulder as it leapt and broke the surface
I could no longer permit the presence in my body
of fictions belonging elsewhere. I pitched my device
then realized my crime against duckweed and all below
I had disowned my own toxicity, poisoned a sanctuary
A wish for telepathy, fallen for dubious shortcomings
Seasons of worry, what of ditches, of jury

12

Closely written pages litter the tale of the avenue along which the woman
doesn't return

Now all we want is a drop of the maiden's blood
A table of cakes or a casket of water, a parenthesis, a leaden
anchor in a garden. The curse read: go to fetch
groceries. What do you make of my dread, she asked
the fortuneteller. A hole in the bottom of your sock
An emptiness so loud even the scratching of a pen impales
Breath underneath sound slipped, a fabric you wear as understory
Glossed, whispered, indrawn like a stitch extracted from lips
Never before had I heard a flute purr. In pine, in fur diagonal
Around her neck a cascade of laced light, a feathered violin
She bows your dream as note after note vanishes to page
Lines her pockets with names, enchants rope
Closely bitten ages flitter, like mail misconstrued, in which the woman
        doesn't unlearn

13

Some say the stars are burning leaves

We can guess that the doll was once dressed in them

when color was harvested from fire, and singed wool

covered wrists. Haunting music hurts your back

Weak impressions merely scratch the page

writing as if the surface were crust and to reach

the mantle required a persistent pressure

not only of intaglio, but of sleight

We're just getting started, placing amber on your absence

A new order took off my hands

The recipient of a lifetime bereavement

award was prohibited from siege

Out the window—thickets of ink

Some say the years are churning eaves

14

(fourteen waning)

This is no way to translate, as if muzzled by the yarn binding the tongue

Sounding sleeves, pristine crossings

Your death is wind talking

An arm extended into the cavern of an empty piano

You were important, impossible, independent

I was hurt, hopeless, the exact words you misspell

Your last name was two brothers

I was the tin flower around her neck

Dear alive creature, I watched your naked hand

Thinking my second choice was best, and then my worst

Only the middle of the photograph appears

recovery of what never happened sits beside you

saying nothing. Must I make it all up?

This is no way to dilate, as if nuzzled by the unborn bridling the sung

14

(fourteen waxing)

She lowers owlets into your arms as if they weren't complete without them

Day after day I composed rows of words which would

not speak to me. My nervousness mounted, amounted to

An enormous or insurmountable absence, punctuated by

dying. As they fall, the leaves guide themselves by light

When you left they were still children, not the fear

of adulthood but the unlikelihood, and the color we

describe (as she hears it in her head). An unrest we

cannot translate. As for the 'grand' in grandmother

I suspect her of reading. Of returning to beginnings

Of receiving the allegorical. Loss would have us revert

to childhood, retrieving nonsense which was never *non sense*

Very vary quite unburied, despite culpability

I know how to stuff myself into the unsaid

She sews eyelets into your charms as if they weren't discretely anthems

15

The train is in fact a curtain air can turn

He set out in his grandfather's coat to magnify
friends, sanctify electric, a song born in a bean field
You left me your breath, called me your mist
I did my crying in private but showed up with eyes absent
and soundless. She pulled the red silk river inside
herself and then laid down beside the tree beings
The music was miscible, a perfect counterpart to language
She liked being in the same noun with kin, kept herself on a short breach
I said 'hi' like a poppy in a root cellar, implied
distance implanted between us so you might miss me
You said 'put me on the map' but what you really wanted
green tea, magenta tea, blue tea
To wane is a pact a certain stare can burn

16

Two roses in the dark, one black and the other invisible

The name of the song is feminine but only for one night

He wore his body on his sleeve, strode amiably into any weather

Face peeled open, features abrupt, hailing a ferryman

You could say reverberation is a gallop, a multiplicity

of bewildering forms, sonorous hounds of spelling

But how to move between your words and your thoughts

Confiscation is the same angel at a desk from every angle

Let me be very clear about running out of letters

I wore none around my neck

We did not show our books in public

Remember this isn't about us, but only our outlines

heaven's own child, lured into a bread house

Blue closing of the park, that lack unprintable

17

A landscape has endless false endings

How to forestall, star before cart

Recline in the middle of an ample face

Dormantly, I sat where I could see you

Aslant ignoring windows full frontal

Smudged with streaks of cloud

Book as filament—cracks along the surface

of an oracle make a fine filigree tree

Signed seasons, scrolled, feigned

I assign you a secret name I dare not pronounce

Maroon hemmed, potent heeled, birds pattering

wet pavement. I wanted to be color but in the end was

swallowed by calm. Blue panic was not wasted

An escape is an endless waltz pending

18

A mother feeds blue candies to a baby

To say it by mouth is simpler

but the hand is more accurate

Though one could not write herself out of time

or power. Lids were drawn against skies

Even if minutes brought nothing to read

I want to trace every one of your lines

I've never been to the spot but I trust you to guide me

Investigating the many paths to misery

Rolling out leaves, mistaking grammar for

gramophone; a correspondence proceeds

by way of etymology. We don't go forward

determining meaning but back into the word

Fragrance of a lure trembling

A shudder feeds blue alleys to a maybe

19

Far ringing air, air foreign, air faring

First I set out to admire your reflection, second
to love, encourage and be rid of you. Then I sought
to beg, barter and betray. I kissed what it was like
to want only what was given, each perfect breath
After epic feign tide I wrote steadily opaque
What I wanted to say I trust you know
An amulet links bodies in time, viscosity
You beside me, a fiction
Listening to unlatched valves inside the poem
Wind, rain and leaves blew up
earlier than air
Hands are cold and hair alights to clouds
Bare wringing air, air florid, air staring

20

Wake up, get married, be born

To love your aesthetics is not the same as to take off
your shirt, pull down your *can't*, lower your friction
To admire your needling is not synonymous
with sun falling fast into neon, nor permission
to open your fingers, spread your hands
through my stare knowing the force of stoic
unkempt sentences. Shoes tumble from
declarations, fledging with fire, steps into ruse
Can you read my affection? Why adamantly
map the place that destroys me?
Aphrodisiac of the impossible
Gone, entirely gone; I can no longer retrieve
fake out, get harried, be sworn

21

Two sacks, sails slack, sadness sinks into the inland saga

A place for everyone in this russet-born frown

I borrowed myself from burrowed wary fruit

Answered to sounds spread by nib

A blotted music first, then gone to harrow

Your name reclined near a series of garments blurred

As arrows darkened night from stark

into sleight—I gazed at your hands

Between your eyes the lit center undone

preserves something, heavily

Heavenly could only be unfastened once

out of clothes, into conundrum

Lives leaning into starry knives

To wax, scales wracked, gladness winks into freehand trauma

22

The very fact of pointing to something commits the person who is pointing

Gravel taller than stars, brown, cosseted

Walk the tired syncopated revolver, ineptitude

A red tree, one flushed finger stretched to glass

What a difference one day makes; so it's over

idiocy remarked, stylus, remnants

Sun, sorrow and turnips should have done more

but still we would not have reached that entire center swath

of country, the ripped up middle between the many shelves

Books, sinks, towns, missives

Endless stones to tell

Sundered in thick silk

So I've always draped, opposed, flattened

The very act of anointing omits the lurking which is painting

23

The vanishing point is vast

Dealings with blacking brush, the unspeakable brought
ashore, placed in a room. They fell asleep and the candles
fell from their hands. And what if I can't. And what if sounds
in the throat humbled sounds of speech mistaken
for love is not. Fallow cement bridges. We blew past
hoping we had surpassed the book that erased
as it fathomed, until I was no longer—an exit
A blur of blue dresses. As for those who thought they had penned me
I stuck pins in their eyes, tore off legs, pulled tunnels along
blasphemous famished rivers. Lights prevent us
from hitting pilings. Voices tempt us to swerve, to turn
to this non-existent you. Collar pulled up, bone to ear
The banishing jaunt is last

But wait, the house lacked a laughing room

Hands knew very well they could not read
despite leaf lights along ledges
The dimly lit was still anywhere inside language
Along rivers colors cannot console
On the way to the opera, in vessels of rain
we witnessed thick books galumphing away
I asked every passerby, quickly amid the new ruin
What must I say to my children? What must we say to our moon?
I dulled my sentence and made my own face
Traced eyed-windows, imperishable fright
Despite staves resembling coffins and whet stones lost
Bridge, bridge break not beneath the bride
What weight—the house lacked a lasting womb

25

We must not underestimate the risk

I made myself scarce, no longer fiction

Speaking in séance I read myself to you

as if I were a book, a ribbon

of text rubbed through your fingers

As if I were no longer

speaking to anyone—sky, ether

Your language no longer coupled with mine

I wish you had not inherited

my silence, my nothing to say

This picture of pen in hand

Our retreat is far from perfect

Gunshots and aircraft populate our eyes

We must rejuvenate our will to ask

The lid of the sun is heavy, its lashes blink on the horizon, brushing the curve of the sea

Darling buds of November will soon be sorry
Winter moth, choose your vocation
Paper wind—damp cocoon
You and your reflection
ran down to the water
Beside the spidered legs of trees
Only hands remain of whereabouts
walk with worry—toward riddle
Braid plus borrow
equals pulse 'we' conceive
nest in chandelier, needles livid
thimbles—infusions of fir
The skid of the stunned is heaven. Crashes brink, blushing the swerve you
      foresee

27

Perhaps we are the victims of false recognition taken by an acquaintance to be a tree

Hand pressed against small of back

Take sunlight as needed, bluebird

and snowflea. Closer than

thought as we change—crowns

with heady wines of gaze

A steadfast shadow ascends stairs

singing. Won by accident, a game

I consent to play only to please others

Because I don't write in words

You gave me a blue cameo

A still face in relief that spoke

For all we did not spindle trees

Perhaps we are prisms—of default apparition—mistaken by contagion—free

28

They took everything away—the nose, the mouth, and then the ears

He spent his best years extracting himself

from shell only to snap back shut

Pliers, razor, scrubbing brush, foam

In the end we had only wings covered

with eyes, your satchel asleep at my feet

like the fog I never acknowledged

Summers lent, refuse tangled at froth

of bed. I found you inside a name

When I tried to approach nearer

the name grew quiet. I lacked

crinkled poppy goblets elixir

strength to lift a coverlet

They mistook everything awake—the rose, the house, and then the years

29

Ghosts are the shadows of knowledge we crave

Inviting electrical impulse, triggers

between waking and rising, the

invisible in which we adorn our selves

Spent an entire buttercup sandwich

(indispensable). So little understood

or embraced beyond words, blue

imaginary billow, oracular

current draws a fragile circle

which is the nether we inhabit

Where we mar each heel struck vast

Bleat, borrow, mend and befriend

I hear the rain inside your vestments

Coaxed are the meadows of solace we engrave

30

She walks awhile unreconciled a hundred miles through chamomile

I spent my time with saplings
astride porcupine caves
My arms were sewn on badly
One season was added for forestalling
and another for neglect. Then he went
wherever he went. From a rope beneath
a house buried, a horse kicking from dirt
Young junipers, thorns in the middle of the trail
Would she allow time to run so far ahead, near
ghost lake, shades of death road, great meadows
walking mist to dark moon bar. Someone
trying to steal the sign, low hanging canopies
Her talk compiled a hundred aisles unrecognized of grand exile

31

I cannot hear except with eyes

Feel free to cry with me, to knock or to balk
Conceive a valance between wary and littoral wife
Less interested in reserve and more in how
to deserve your attention. I'll take pleading
vehicular language strung in a bottomless race
Not difficult at first, but the years that follow summon
until you fall to hazard. Your accusation: I had not *told* my *telling*
Your calling was neither beneath awnings nor worth confiding
So you set out on your way to market with a basket on your arm
Wind blew permissions against fretting. You said you were not
making decisions only opening doors to see which were invitations
The opposite of unfollowing or to follow where nothing leads—
I cannot disappear except in guise

32

Dear reader, were you ever a girl

What is the name which when uttered alters you unendingly?

Do you trust your given hands? Don't say the wasting is lovely

as in only one kind of candor. Never before our wedded pangs

Which is the room you return to without

assistance or choice? Don't say, I know how you kneel

because you couldn't possibly plough. Is your body that room?

Don't offer ablation, unproven reason, laurels or borders

So that a picture becomes an hour to embalm

or embed, a daughtered sphere, what not to say

Don't mask the vow you are, any name by which you call me

Don't stalk declarations, even those faring spells

Offer, bliss, bless, and also their messenger

Near seer will you ever unfurl?

33

Unrhyming in the present but rhyming in the past

Bled paper is humble

When light changes we range

Does an ocean have seasons?

The exact date is not ill. The stricken

require courage while the fainting stay

home. It's true we contain a skyline

and a river, exist on a torn page. A face

turns to the side. Covers eyes with hair

So much affection for a face I cannot see

We elect ourselves as relevant culprits, determinants

One hand warming the other but both hands were sad

Unhinging the hesitant, hammering in the past

Pleating the sheet, hour by hour

You will only know the unknowable here

That is, you aren't allowed to ask

Asking is crossing a line where one life becomes another

You enter, making a room and all of its inhabitants exist

A body which radiates seems to wave as it approaches

Arms outstretched, outspoken, mining—what next

A face opens as an articulation of a message received

Write the unspoken rules

Where all bodies are fluid

Between presence and intimation of form

We must forget our true endings

Assemble beginnings

Pleasing the street, power by power

35

There was once a young woman who late in life grew a second, small, superfluous
tongue under the first, but she could find no purpose for it and from lack of use it
soon withered away

I held the two words in my mouth
Not names or actions yet they signaled new relations
Intaglio daughters were born from absence
From staring at what does not yet exist
Admiration etched in glass or stone
A face invented is a face inverted
I unfollowed her gracious apology to purslane and grouse
Because I didn't know how to make your absence
disappear I strung shells around my neck, plucked
forgetfulness to adorn a ravaged town, prayed
for Bana Alabed in bomb strewn Aleppo, with 222,000 followers
Ghost trains empty of sympathy, full of skepticism
There was once an unsung human who late in life grew a second, small,
obstreperous book lung under the first, but she could find no usurpers for it
       and from lack of juice it soon slithered away

All prancing proud horses sweat milk and are mothered by low-lying clouds

Where wolf speaks to wainscot

berths of water are assembled from light

Ink reddens between sleeping and waking

Tentative dancers inscribe filigree waists

Solitude requires the company of those absent

You were ever, nether, or never

If nothing else you knew how to say goodbye

Ask anyone's wildness to speak to wilderness

The new language we call magnificence

is silence, a fragrant wreath with ancestral candle center

Nearness is an intoxicating land

All chanson sown sources fret milk and are mothered by low-flying vowels

37

There were not enough faces in the mirror for her selves

Until the moment he drew their curve

she was not aware she possessed shoulders

One moment she fell into his aura

a large pit far better than firewood

The next moment nothing but silence fell

between them in thick resinous sheaves

As if he were reciting the thousand reasons

he would never belong to goats ears of emperors

rocks eating breakfast, she, his sister, servant or end

She turned off bloodflow to all probable windows

Wrote by hand—*meeting after a long*

absence I want to remember who you are

There were not enough ages in the quiver for her wells

As a child, on a bed, at the starting gate, even today—imagine it

Handwritten womb, tremors the color red

When asked to inscribe the title you look up

why the jellyfish has no shell, an entire illegible

page, pleasure in waves like a romantic notion keeps

you—company along the poem lined streets

Diagrams in lobes, entranceways, a blue dress face down

on a bed, head hidden, washed up every day on a beach

light rubbed into bloom, lips tremble

A bird looks at itself in a mirror with binoculars

I wrote by candlelight with the door closed for as long as I wanted

In simple curves with pockets for pencils and scraps

of vapor, crickets, dried flowers, dead parentheses around neck

Beguiled, on a thread, at the parting gate, reason astray—imagine it

O thorns of the black bougainvillea, fronds of the purple palm, you have thrust
your shadows into the garden of my friend

Alone in a gestating language, describe pleasure from inside
the body. Lying in bed, poems beneath back; eyes in palms
of hands, and the eye between eyes lit. Bedsheets like fictions
fall into hearsay. Is this a letter or is this a story?
Are we of flesh or are we of flight?
Many words were spoken and the words caressed
other words, coaxed them to enter. Still others watched
the door, the inner voice, or were not brave enough
to take off their coats. Dropped from shoulders to paper roads
Interiors spreading like ink, auras stuffed with lace resistance
Happiness is one ingredient of sadness. Sadness is one ingredient
of living—in multiple. Brightness is what the bare trees are saying
     against the very slight blushing of snow
O arms lack insignias, bonds of the fertile dawn, you have trussed your repose
     into the pardon of my pen

The prairie undulates as if there were only a single mind to which one goes for one's thoughts

They stole from themselves under the guise of otherworldly
sewn orphans, ferret to shoulder, goose under arm
Their first robbery was oxygen, daybreak, headless gazelles
sleep, a dust heap, three princes and their conceits
a body in a cellar, a wooden helpmeet, peach blossom's quarrel
When they walked out wolves protected their weeping
They stole rays of the sun and with their voice
they kept you warm. Once upon a time the unhappened
spoke: Bake a loaf of bread—to keep tongue brave
Give your beloved: twins with molten hours
Bury yourself in earth up to your neck. You, thief of beauty
will have no rest even in your grave
the prayer undulates as if there were only a single bind transposed for
      one's aughts

41

Long ago I was once in Seville in a blue dress that could be washed and dried
in ten minutes

Does one see or hear the echo of the naked figure exiting the cistern?

Is it better to say or to stay?

Often or soften?

Ask the cards—or is that foolish?

What do I mean?

A crown and bells for the one most late to breakfast

Ribbon, medals, wreaths, applause

Can you capture listening instead of sonority?

Discarding old selves, hung from Yggdrasil tree?

What is the tone of your timbre

when running toward cliffs and abandonment?

Do you seek the very bottom of resonance?

A song ago I was dissed and distilled in a rue dress that could be lost and
        cried in ten minutes

Only hearing, taking no other action, one deracinates

Two images of birth, the daughter of cups before the ten

of swords, underestimated appointments with sky

Stinting words, expecting midwife, or the couple

in bed, each writing a document of their love

A scientific paper (xxx likes xxx), a poem, or a diagram of

each movement; messages wrought severe claustrophobia

Dear search-yourself, please stop—he reached for all lawless

resources but could not wake a better word for bedlam

Angst exits one body and migrates to another

When I learned that persons take on disguises

We hung our names

In that nether where we are anyone

Only wearing, mapping no other attraction, one gravitates

43

Language is as blind as sleep

Imbroglio daughters, imbroglio mind

tried to sneak up on cognition

to see what one can only see

after years in proximity

to any person, only human

celebrity subsides, we see underside

the shift, dim spots. Our adoration absurd

We yell, get out of my imbroglio mind, but too late

We fall for disease or glamour when not yet

believable as animals unrehearsed

Please help—I want to be free of this carcass

Mistaking beloved for consummation

Language unkind and steep

The witch of the micro-wilderness between minutes lifts her fist and counterpunches

Your etchwork a tree, commonly cleared

hollows, caverns ruined, malefic

Inscribed on calendar—every blink

No one wants to be known by wax or clay features

I sat in a corner scrying beside a ladder

scuffed trunk asking—why so easily do we love

quick incorrect answers, all of them planted

become permanent, not placeholders

significant zeros, cunning syntax dismantled

tree toppled—she screwed herself in anew

You wanted to see me?

Before you were born, said the cottage to the child

A stitch of retro-wilderness between minuets pierces lip and crosshatches

If a woman were to rhyme district *with* compact *would she have time, would she follow her daughters*

Buckling chrysalis in search of nothing
A wordless receiving of verbs
Woven instructions for sublime unrest
Do you like your new body or name
sewn, blended, torn, superimposed
Meaning is lent; auras wave green
Where brew is sly gone astray
Would you like some coiled medicine
Seedlings of the instantaneous
We are daunting; we are deigning; we are darning
Long since I've had a family or lived in a book
She took the hood off of her goose, braced herself
If a woman were to rhyme *explicit* with *enact* would she halve thyme, would
    she follow her augur

46

I cannot play the instrument of lamentation, it's impossible to tune

What blankness may not secure soft detours may attain
If this farce does not recede there still remains the
discourse of doors, moors, fires, stars oars, cures
Even emperors are only men we want to enter. Centers
quite intractable. The empress expressed herself in dissent
Tried to extract herself but was first straddled, then swallowed
Mentor of consent sent misrepresentations, anon polyphonic
driving clothes around. Backdrops disappear in silenced bodies
On which paper would you write to your idol?
Shoulders pressed without a word
The night is dark and we in it secret, a first song
I cannot sway the dissonance of initiation, irreconcilable moon

47

It isn't time that takes each new night away and returns the old day and puts
a period to our desires

Is prose a continuous thought implausible to break
or are we speaking about the spinal solemn and born
broken into bones, fleet passages, reveries prone
Your breath fitted beside mine, shoulders near and almost
inside hands, knees, the way you moved, contorted
Across from 'my' as if to throw back your torso
Unplug your legs and force them back into sockets
Hips rolling under graciousness, a certain gravity
Elysium, after light, fortunate fields, shade parks
Stirred, translations made me cry not attached
to bodies but to the ideal or idea of an emotional
replica that enacts a ritual we inscribe
It isn't rhyme that takes each new height away, returns the quay, and plays
     our myriad hours

48

The sunlight has lit silver quivers on the rosemary—it has so many aromatic fates

Give up youth inside partnered electric ledges

We prepare for our death in certain documents

In order to not think about it we live in a book

on a page, in our work, in other faux fantasies

Or do we go as beggars, masking the most ornate

sadness—until we suddenly saw time as a chrysalis

Like the change of mood the midwife described

before transition. How can you tell I'm not close

—No one had examined me

More afraid than clever

I came here to inhabit the emptiness I rely on

A blank room with tall ceilings and moldings, a chandelier-fireplace

Midnight slit mirrors on the wary—so many cinematic gates

49

See style, *see* working late, *see* mismatched socks, *see* polyphony

A child-bearing woman is born into a future source

She will be human but almost unknown to herself

We've walked in that rain you rarely understand

Uncountable, beyond body or name

More intimate than mating, unhinged

Without link to time or slight

But then sinking lower and lowly

Not liking you one little bit while at the same time

Wanting to take a bite of your fate

Wade into the edges of form—dissolve into nether

Until we stitch ourselves back into determinate

Walk into a new day feigned

See *smile,* see *lurking bait,* see *unattached clocks,* see *epiphany*

50

After the river of your inlet withdraws, sound, sing to ground

We covered your body with stripped cloth

Dined on your person adorned with flowers

Supposed we had to walk outside ourselves

So stepped back (from and inside transparencies)

So you were flown around; so you disguised

your features with tethers. So you waded into

indiscreet thickets where you could become someone

other. So I said the word 'whorl' and then

'furred' but not the word 'hurled' not the noun

Not your body, not below cloth and ash

Irreplaceable—I don't want to say goodbye

to beginning, which is always the easiest ending

After the giver of your inset resounds, comes round, rings found

51

An allegory is a depiction of something that can't be depicted

You advised me to pierce each kernel with lightly

smoked needle, stabbed straight through the start

to avoid breakage—but rupture was my aspiration

To revel in disintegration—do I tell you who I am?

Music falling on the body, blue eventuality

Licking azure fomentations—asleep

Do I coagulate, radiate, concentrate

Her coat of curled adjectives, borders in mouth

How to keep the exact distance required

Nearness scored, precise heat of heaven

That ahead of us—which was once fathoms

recedes between cusps

Our malady is an eviction of something that can't be encrypted

52

The old white woman in the long black skirt pauses at the kitchen sink, struck by sudden consciousness

How are you?—*old* (says the mundane sun)

I had to endure it or it had to endure me

But now—prepare your walls

She spoke in throats of all seasons

He thought: if only someone across the sea

would secretly weep upon hearing my verses

A long flocked skirted series of lines

Unable to live without plasma of affectionate letters

Strewn across the naked floor of your art

Never mine, nevermind unmaking symptoms

Plug me in to some scarce source

Alone in a room of my own mistaking

The bold bright human in the wrong hack smirk rises to the hitch and brink,

    plucked by hidden hands, sonorous

53

Clouds awaiting captions

O how unlucky! Where can I be?

Is there no one to show me out of this wood?

Only a red ball in the brain of a calf

A ribbon mouth beneath a pale cloud lit the land

A portrait made at exorbitant cost

Less and less about a series of in and out breaths

Go, ordered the goblin, drink up the brook

In a soundless world your voice dies in your throat

Water rushes noiselessly over pebbles; hair stands like bristles

The prince crept into the kennel and began darning socks

With this plait I bind your mouth

With this peg I keep you still

Brows abating matches

54

An ink man on paper, a chalk man on a sidewalk, and a shadow man, a sleeping
man, an ash man, a man of bones—well, they don't scare me

At what venture did I give up temerity in favor
of your hand, abandon counting wolves in the 'would'
At what fork did I inadvertently choose an iron shovel red-hot
When did 'once' become a barely discernible silk
thread bound to the foreleg of a series of waving lines
A path of future smears on a face
How might we follow them: blue ash, green stain
When did I succumb to occluded charm
Your solvent voice as an antidote to onlyness
Unfallen accidents pause in a corridor
Were we more bereft or immune to the passage
She lit the candles in her face, and then her fate
A brink woman on vapor, a locked woman on a bridewalk, and a photo
      woman, a keeping woman, an eyelash woman, a woman of unknowns—
      well, they don't spare me

55

If vacillation of mind is to continue, we must skate deeper, upholding delighted
skulls

In multi-compositional fields you find more privacy

Your back to the boy who seduces every person he ever meets

An emotive white field strains eyes bisected

Every statement is cut off in the novel one cannot

domesticate or possess— When you are 'fine' the day opens

immediately not doing what I said, not sitting at desk

I saw what was solid when I saw them together

Pausing from what you would call the sturdy inner iris

To tell first the poet who pulled me across an ocean

Second—hypnotized a room. Her name was *Plea* but we called her *Quell*

Third—sat beside me and whispered one last thermostat, caveat potions

Invented a secret language in which to incite

If aspiration unsigned is to continue, we must scrape deeper, unfolding

ignited hulls

56

By moving from window to window and carefully recording at each what we see,
we...

En route along a farsighted wooden pier we walked
plied by stride to an ecstatic cerulean happening. As we
approached we saw numerous jade persons seated
cross-legged facing the wide ochre ocean with notebooks
in crimson silence waiting for the arrival of music
An archive which would emerge in the form of color wafting
in from the charcoal sea. Each figure poised to receive
otherworldly plainsong. To transcribe silver and celadon
canticle lights, rare magenta elements, cadmium, boundless
Our bodies coral as we approach sienna
Would each composition be identical azure
Or is reception as unique as violet tracery
By moving from crescendo to pillow and carefully cording at each what we
     plea, we...

57

In the stiff air, down the unbalanced wind, over dusty culverts, women bear their hot cells of benevolence

Written in a closet because it would not wait
Sage is escorted away from childhood
and then the youngest days of your children
until you lose recognition of tarmac
She was thinking precisely incorrect thoughts
to forget primary rife ferried
without consent, without admonition
One could say her entire life up to that moment
had been so sufficiently obfuscated she could
not see it while she scrawled in the closet
Many tried to coax her out, but her need
was urgent—a spectacular hunger
In glyph dares, gowned and talented skin over smudged overtures, women
snare their sought spells of pre-eminence

She as she, splendid as sand spun into glass

There must be something other than a gestural

method for fleeing what we bear

as we rip at weft—as we fray

Absent of all constrictions

Dauntless, beyond blindness

In the middle of my shelf is a strange ground

Wish, stagger, quiver, crepuscular

Awnings, constancy, conjugation, repetition

Imperturbable consort of the invisible

To speak fluently *our* language

(that such a language might exist)

One vast inflection, in the middle of glyph

Sea as scree, suspended as a hand stunned into brass

59

It is early morning in the late Cretaceous

And if I were to end a book with GO BACK

A cow was once a fish was once a worm

I was a sluggish ancestor, from bison, an auroch

In woolly mammoth time dire wolves roamed

Rude trolls rode, favored saber tooth bats

Truth or neighborhood, worst pet skulls

Did words evolve from letters, from sill, syllabary

Numbers evolved from cabbages, aimed first

in fields, days, fingers. Hands evolved from ask

Smoke evolved from cinder cats, veins from flask

Candles evolved from eyes, incendiary innuendos

Villains named something that does not evolve

Early forewarning in the late audacious

Wren in ragged bee line, flora sleeping live

In time I learned the difference between true

flora and flowery, between the thousand

kisses and consolation. The uncanny

was in your smile. Let's dance this edge

as long as we can which only exists

by virtue of mutual interest

If we cross, broach, press, a chasm collapses

(so the cliff face no longer resists)

If we dross, undress, assemble

Here—rip this effigy to shreds

And I was a leaden curtain

Let us not uncross our skies

Again in tacit shine, aurora sweeping hive

61

The egg is milk at rest and an orb under asymmetrical conditions

Forestalling Elysian lanes

as if one could think in seams

ruined by every effaced trail

leads to a rare globular countryside

adorned pause, anarchy tavern, mayhem

A *soon* we sing in rye, *handmead*

made secret—a name for amen

Anthems by middle moon

in tiny spiral night, a notebook

we hide legibly in almost

magenta, inmost, voice of

tree inscribes sky—

To beg is ilk at breast, a verb wandering, alchemical premonitions

62

This dirty Venus, this resemblance to nothing we knew of the dead

Your life is not the path you choose nor in accomplishments
When you hold up one hand delimiting mirror and the other
a picture you suppose you are to inhabit
then look from one to the other in disappointment
you must know that even your own hands have lied
If you place one atop another laced with mine between
or one to chest the other to hold the first in place against gravity—
Things to do with hands which act as perplexing mirrors
Press palms into ground to bear weight
Press hands together and they form each one to another
or better yet if your hands tend, cook or knit, if nothing worse
instruct your hands with subtle speech—began the story gone mad
    in a mirror
This early Venus, this semblance to blunting we drew from the said

63

Have I not nematodes in my gut, have I not delusions in my brain, have I not
white blood in my veins

Write it in a way in which it could be anyone
you've ever thrown away only to realize your mistake
Come closer your own sleep keeps you
or would you rather stay where you are
When you want nothing more than to be taken
into the arms of—fire laughed, hearths died
A little pane through which they could see nothing
beckoned moss, stone, table, sunset, a single lake
disenchanted from all keys, halls and horses
I've already had a proper life and now I want another
night, valence, molecules unpaired, ink of presentiment
You in upper right corner atop a blue border—I dreamed your name
Have I not roads in my thrust, have I not transfusions in my bane, have I not
    polite floods in my remains

64

Actually, I am not addressing myself here to metaphysicians, nor to spirits,
nor to pedants, because none of these know how to see the particular beauty
of a rain-soaked field

Have you ever pitched a dialectic priestess
In travel we become anyone
A coat disappearing into ceaseless talk
A gold copse of trees to obscure proclivities
I stopped myself from errors of tattered completion
Replaced myself on a shelf, unbound my laces
Wrote the morning as it ascended
blue behind branches, drawn from sky
pleasure between severed reflections
weightless alibis, an unspoken promise
like a trellis a foresight to touch
A face opens and you bathe in light
Actually, I am not confessing myself here to suspicions, nor to coherence,
        nor to penance, because none of these know how to please the
        particular brood of a stain-stroked shield

65

Cat in the redwood, chasing pie

I must learn to speak to myself more severely

as stitching of history dissolves

the gone is nearly transparent

ecstatic-platonic run clockwise swinging

A parade of paper balls to frighten winter

strings circling like maces

Before missives, before wand and asphyxiation

Opens a fictional door, a crowded yellow blanket

Sewing names into our coats

Time to rid ourselves of all mystic floors

danger of selves suddenly close

unfolding rhetoric and beds

Thermostat in threadblades, chasing 'try'

You disappear into a duration

I wrote what I remembered of our meeting

then placed my face inside notebook

close to the lettering until words

touched my cheek and all other sounds

dimmed—strawsong, pulling

Queries, red-wrapped

A lovely cubicle we enter

Appetites, compartments, rubbing

against interruption, distraction

Sorry, lorry and slurry, we come apart

Message cures curvature

Finally I'm convinced: pinpricks, lines, hooks

You persevere into pulsation

Serene is the soot far up the chimney

Sutt, sažda, huzel, chimley

Sleep forces animals to lie still and forget, forge

hearth, follow lava into glass, explosive oceans

Furnished by furnace—our synapses grew exuberantly by day

I'd rather not be a part of your collection of fingered

trinkets though I was told it is impolite to boil

water in two eggshells or refuse an invitation of this kind

Hollow, we were escorted out of the mountain

When we laugh it will all be over

We are as old as the forest but have never made a book

of ephemera, stacks of stray pages, wandering desks

mistakes, unneeded copies, research, drafts, all of it found

Arcane is the 'could' which leads us dimly

Past tense, present tense, three legs in a single brown shoe

Dear sedated daughter—surrender

to waters end, lanced air

Restore scold shed remnant

Did you love every friend or befriend love

For she unlike disenchantment

found worse than palest pressure

Dawn bisected

I should have met you at the name

Blue beneath contour

Circles of major arcana

Silent tendriled animal cusped

Hollow bodies of sounds unspoken

Past sense, present suspense, three dregs in a single drowned clue

69

In the city of music stands a fountain of pitches

I rewrite the silence, hit send

Close anoint—cannot cover loss

Clothes bury budding instruments

Favor nimbleness over armor

Quiet staggering crises

Not only ecology created this forest

A star was dying straight overhead, decay

Cobalt—cloudlike signals hidden by dust

Amphibians wake from winter sleep

Migrate to vernal pools, breed

Some travel by wind, unseen by humans

Some travel by woods where others cross factual streets

In the lily of musing stands a mountain of stitches

Resolute as the canyon oak, she branches, then leaves

Fine print as epic tale tinctured

Without the need for voluminous program notes

Given sonic texture

Newcomer sound, mourning

A moaning bow eerily

droning lasso like

I dress and undress until I approach

or resemble myself

Magnetic yields spin and sweep

like the beam of a lighthouse

A shredded star resembles a string of pearls

radiating more energy than one hundred million tongues

Resolute as stranded smoke, launches, then weaves

71

The silver river is irreversible but you attentively watch its mouth

Open foliate night, send footsteps far

Unfasten gem, letter, frame

The bewildered mirror is vestigial

yet you legibly search its vows

Mercury fingers, succinct

Blight pillaged skirts

Broom and shadow

Shrug between sutures, startle bone

Every rupture a complicit lunation

Inside skin, dusk ushers pavement

glitter, unmentionable lips

A crossbow scuds over glass; contrast stands still

The silver fissure is inescapable yet you inventively arch aloud

O, there is a blading in this gentle bend

A candle flame she stood alone, solstice

in her lap, a harp, their park, his parse

Night pulled ink around our clocks, hidden hearths

Literature was still a pageant, wintering

over shrouds, veins, sinews, and necklacing

At echoes pledge, a mock thrall rises, a monument

to pleasure. Have you ever met viridian

like a noun with sandpaper and tomorrow's involuntary

rumor—breath dipped in swamp-rest

unknowable beyond our frail manipulative

hours, earthly surprises, flight

Nothing matters here, except in reflection

Know, there is a braiding in our disassembled ascent

73

Pillage, pilfer, weep, digress

Meet me this night

in nether rooms

beneath the rose

or better yet, unnamed

Where is the constant present

(first line, or partial)

Our next rule (entirely found)

Dare to ignore: I've been unwell

If only burning eyes invoked

powers. We need a title or could be a draft

One in a series of cities, myriads of

sessions kissing paintings

Look through a window, turn right

Pillow, wither, heap, distress

74

Writers dowse in books

Woken from first or second
earth, mineral sleep
Injured thoughts recur in tree
We remarked on colors
of the sky, and former lives
Not everything was stolen
Page upon page you wove
wells through my hair
willows. A balcony slept in a wide
brimmed hat, a reunion
pushing back a chair
dearest now, eves of spinning clocks
liars espouse in looks

75

I could plunge through the hole in my tongue

I said to the teacup I should be patient
filled with hypericum perforatum
warming lips and mouth
fleeing over an apparition
infusing hands with liquid names
Your art, to meet in air, música sacra
ethereal climates, winged blue
buttons, diamond strutted post-death
Materials we assemble at the end of already
A crack in the neck of a comet
Small unbelievable patches of snow stranded
Death of ex-adjectives
I could smudge through the coal in my lung

76

A woman I'll name another day

Ignoring a needle, courting thread

How to help an underthought

know nothing before scrawl

not even how to draw breath in lines

White skies, dirges persist

every stab at—daughtering

How to love motherless words

What shall we say to the well meaning, clueless

not yet born. How to stand, dress, speak

before retiring names (letters, skirmish, flight)

Having once been a person reading the wrong books

I won't say that which unfastens margins

A woman in flames another way

77

I've no other sentence to speak, to syntax, to serve

My mind was a thief—consciousness wept

over where it had not followed itself

unfollowing instead a series of uncertain

sonatas, movements written in barely

discernible creases in your forehead

You departed. I had never learned sight-reading

I searched the non-existent brows of trees

furrows of sky, further nouns, castings of leafy

silence, autobiographical carmine, strings parting

I sought captioned incandescence, was led to numberless

winters, syntax of vigilant suns, sentenced clocks

grandmothers unfolding visibility in hammocks of fog

I've no other sentience to streak, to climax, to curve

Notes

Intaglio Daughters is an homage text for the poet Lyn Hejinian. All titles (in italics above each poem) are taken from her book *The Unfollowing*. In the preface to her book she writes "I wanted each line to be as difficult to accept on the basis of the previous and subsequent lines as death is for we who are alive—a comparison that I make intentionally, since my intention in writing the sequence of poems I'm calling 'The Unfollowing' was to compose a set of elegies." In considering a form for *Intaglio Daughters* I wondered—what follows loss and rupture? What follows unfollowing? The mourning process often involves a non-sequential experience of time—and many returns, wavelike, in spirals or contractions. In keeping with this idea of rounds, sinuous or labyrinth-time, reaching backward and forward simultaneously, my book is a series of rondels, with the final line in each poem returning to, and resounding Hejinian's language.

Acknowledgments

Grateful acknowledgment to the following editors, and to the journals where excerpts of these poems first appeared: *Boog Lit, Boneless Skinless, Dispatches, Flag + Void, Lute & Drum, Under a Warm Green Linden,* and *YesPoetry.* Thank you to Mel Bentley, Michael Bough, Buck Downs, Logan Fry, Caroline Gormley, David Kirschenbaum, Kent Johnson, Jonathan Hamilton, Matthew Moore, Pete Moore, Christopher Nelson, Ken Taylor & Joanna Valente. Thank you to Lee Ann Brown, Kate Colby, Patricio Ferrari, Sarah Riggs and Lisa Jarnot, for readings, conversations and encouragement. Thank you to Lyn Hejinian whose work and generous presence is a tremendous gift and inspiration. Many thanks to Mark Harris of Ornithopter Press.

About the Author

Laynie Browne's recent books include a collection of poems, *Translation of the Lilies Back into Lists* (Wave Books, 2022) and the anthology *A Forest on Many Stems: Essays on The Poet's Novel* (Nightboat Books, 2021). Honors include a Pew Fellowship, the National Poetry Series Award, and the Contemporary Poetry Series Award. She teaches and coordinates the MOOC Modern Poetry at University of Pennsylvania.

www.ingramcontent.com/pod-product-compliance
Lightning Source LLC
Chambersburg PA
CBHW022201080426
42734CB00006B/530